10/19/04

Questions and Answers: Countries

France

by Kremena Spengler

Consultant:
Frank A. Anselmo, PhD
Department of French Studies
Louisiana State University
Baton Rouge, Louisiana

Capstone press
Mankato, Minnesota

Fact Finders is published by Capstone Press
151 Good Counsel Drive, P.O. Box 669, Mankato, Minnesota 56002
www.capstonepress.com

Library of Congress Cataloging-in-Publication Data
Spengler, Kremena.
    France / by Kremena Spengler.
    p. cm.—(Fact finders. Questions and answers: Countries)
    Includes bibliographical references and index.
    ISBN 0-7368-2689-0 (hardcover)
    1. France—Juvenile literature. [1. France.] I. Title. II. Series.
DC17.S69 2005
944—dc22   2003026239

Summary: A brief introduction to France, following a simple question-and-answer format
    that discusses land features, government, housing, transportation, industries, education,
    sports, art forms, holidays, food, and family life. Includes a map, fast facts, and charts.

Editorial Credits
Megan Schoeneberger, editor; Kia Adams, series designer; Jennifer Bergstrom, book
    designer; maps.com, map illustrator; Wanda Winch, photo researcher; Scott Thoms,
    photo editor; Eric Kudalis, product planning editor

Photo Credits
Bruce Coleman Inc./J-C Carton, 4, 11; John Elk III, 12–13, 27
Capstone Press Archives, 29 (top)
Corbis/Archivo Iconografico, S.A., 21; Ludovic Maisant, 9; Owen Franken, 15; Royalty Free,
    cover (background), 1; Will and Deni McIntyre, 17
Doranne Jacobson, 23
Folio Inc./Katherine Karnow, 25
Getty Images Inc./AFP, 8; Doug Pensinger, 18–19; Hulton Archive, 6, 7
StockHaus Limited, 29 (bottom)
Zuma Press/Colorise/Money, cover (foreground)

Artistic Effects
Ingram Publishing, 16; Truffle and Truffe/Le Caveur, les Produits d'un Terroir, 24

1 2 3 4 5 6 09 08 07 06 05 04

Table of Contents

Features

Where is France?

France is a country in western Europe. It is about the size of the U.S. state of Texas.

Plains make up most of France. In some places, low **plateaus** break up the plains.

France also has hilly areas. The Massif Central is in south central France. This landform has rounded hills and deep valleys.

Pine forests grow in the foothills of the Alps mountain range. ▶

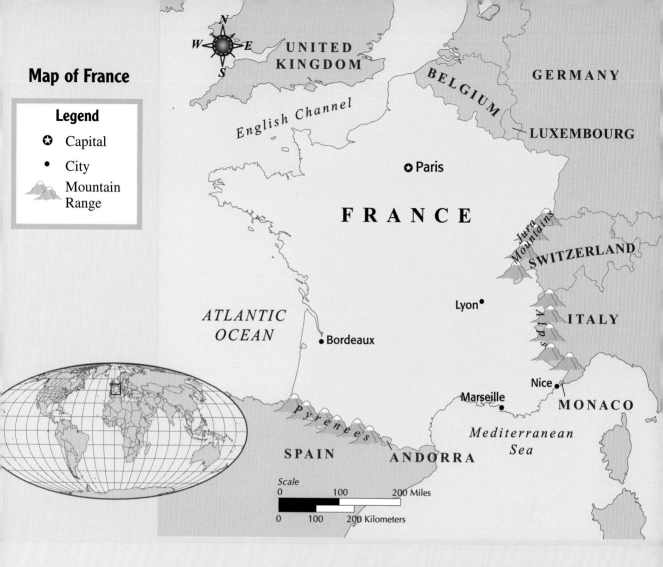

Map of France

Legend

- ✪ Capital
- • City
- 🏔 Mountain Range

UNITED KINGDOM

BELGIUM

GERMANY

LUXEMBOURG

English Channel

✪ Paris

FRANCE

Jura Mountains

SWITZERLAND

ATLANTIC OCEAN

Lyon•

Alps

ITALY

• Bordeaux

Nice•

MONACO

Marseille•

Mediterranean Sea

Pyrenees

SPAIN

ANDORRA

Scale

0   100   200 Miles

0   100   200 Kilometers

Tall mountains stretch along France's eastern and southern borders. The snowy Alps border Italy. The Jura Mountains border Switzerland. The Pyrenees divide France from Spain.

When did France become a country?

France became a country in the late 400s. People called Franks settled in the area now known as France. A ruler named Clovis united the people and called the area Francia.

Powerful kings ruled France for hundreds of years. Their rule ended with the French **Revolution** in 1789.

King Clovis was the first king of France. ➤

The French people attacked the state prison, the Bastille, starting the French Revolution.

The French people were upset with the king. They attacked the state prison, the Bastille. They won this first fight against the king. After years of battle, the French finally overthrew their king. In 1792, they changed the government.

What type of government does France have?

France is a **republic**. In a republic, the people vote for their leaders. French voters must be at least 18 years old.

France has a president. The president chooses a **prime minister** and signs treaties. The prime minister works with the **parliament**.

The French prime minister gives a speech to parliament. ▶

The French parliament meets to pass laws.

Parliament meets in Paris, France's capital. The parliament has two groups. The National Assembly makes laws. The Senate gives suggestions and ideas to the National Assembly.

What kind of housing does France have?

Houses are common in small cities and towns. Many people in France own their homes. Most homes have indoor toilets, showers or baths, and central heating. Air conditioning is not common.

Where do people in France live?

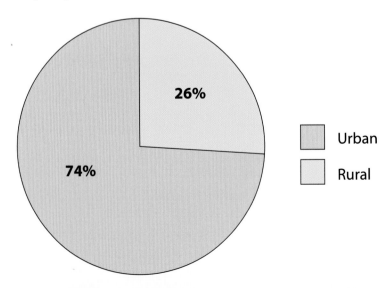

26%

74%

Urban

Rural

French houses are often large.

In large cities, many people live in apartments. Some old buildings have been made into apartments. Some people live in modern high-rise apartments.

What are France's forms of transportation?

In cities, people use public transportation. They ride buses, subways, or streetcars. Many people ride trains between cities. High-speed trains called TGVs run between many French cities. These trains travel at 186 miles (300 kilometers) per hour.

France's roads provide ways to move goods across the country. Some highways include tunnels to pass through mountains.

Fact!

The Channel Tunnel allows people to take a train from France to England under the English Channel. The tunnel is known as the Chunnel.

People use TGVs and other trains to travel between cities.

France has many airports. About 76 million people visit France each year. Orly and Charles de Gaulle airports near Paris are very busy. Other cities, such as Marseille, Nice, and Lyon, also have large airports.

What are France's major industries?

Services, such as hotels and restaurants, make up a large part of France's **economy**. Most French workers have service jobs.

French workers make many products. They make machines, electronics, and chemicals. Renault and Peugeot-Citroen are large carmakers. France is a world leader in aircraft and space rockets. The French also make clothing, perfumes, and leather goods.

What does France import and export?	
Imports	*Exports*
crude oil	*aircraft*
machinery and equipment	*machinery*
vehicles	*plastics*

Farmers harvest grapes for wine in northern France.

France has rich farmland. Farmers grow wheat, corn, sugar beets, and grapes. They raise cattle, pigs, and chickens. The French also make hundreds of cheeses.

What is school like in France?

In most French schools, the school day starts at 8:30 in the morning. It ends at 4:30 in the afternoon. Lunch break lasts 90 minutes.

French children must go to school from age 6 to 16. For the first five years, they go to primary school. From age 11 to 15, they attend a middle school. In France, middle school is called collége.

Fact!

French students do not have school on Wednesdays. Instead, they go to school on Saturday mornings.

French students get a long lunch break.

After middle school, students choose a lycée. This school is like a senior high school. A lycée prepares students for a difficult test. Students must pass this test if they want to go to a university.

What are France's favorite sports and games?

Bicycle racing is a big sport in France. Every July, people gather for the Tour de France. Hundreds of cyclists race for three weeks through France and neighboring countries. People line the streets to cheer them on.

Soccer is popular in France. People watch games on TV. France hosted the World Cup Soccer games in 1998. That year, the French team won its first world title.

Fact!

The Rally Paris-Dakar is a famous and difficult car race. It starts in Paris and crosses the Sahara Desert in Africa.

Racers round a corner in the Tour de France bicycle race.

Boules (BOOL) is a popular game in France. In southern France, it is known as *pétanque* (pay-TAHNK). Players roll or throw metal balls at a smaller ball.

What are the traditional art forms in France?

For hundreds of years, France has been a center for arts. Many famous painters have come from France. Claude Monet, Edgar Degas, and Pierre-Auguste Renoir are well-known French painters.

France is also known for its writers. French books, such as *The Hunchback of Notre Dame* by Victor-Marie Hugo and *The Three Musketeers* by Alexandre Dumas, are still read today.

Fact!

People from around the world visit France's museums, especially the Louvre in Paris. The Louvre is one of the world's largest art museums.

Claude Monet created this painting of water lilies.

French classical music is also popular. Claude Debussy and Maurice Ravel are famous composers. Georges Bizet's *Carmen* is one of the world's most often performed and filmed operas.

What major holidays do people in France celebrate?

The French celebrate their national holiday, Bastille Day, on July 14. People celebrate this day with parades, fireworks, and street dances.

Some holidays in France are Christian, including Christmas and Easter. On Christmas Eve, people go to midnight church services. Children receive gifts from Father Christmas. On Easter, children receive candy eggs and chocolate chickens. They hunt for Easter eggs.

What other holidays do people in France celebrate?

Armistice Day
Good Friday
Labor Day
New Year's Day

Some people wear costumes for Bastille Day celebrations.

St. Nicholas Day is another favorite holiday. St. Nicholas Day begins the night of December 5. Some children put their shoes out for St. Nicholas. Good children find them filled with gifts. Naughty children get a stick from Father Whip.

What are the traditional foods of France?

The French are famous for their fine food. A large meal includes soup, a main course, salad, cheese, and dessert. Steak with french fries and roast chicken with vegetables are popular main courses. Favorite foods are goose liver spread, frog legs, and snails. Fruit tarts and cream-filled pastries are French desserts.

Fact!

Black, warty mushrooms called truffles are an expensive French food. People eat truffles in salads or omelettes. People use dogs and pigs to sniff truffles out of tree roots.

A man sells loaves of bread called baguettes at a French bakery.

France is known for long thin loaves of bread called baguettes. Baguettes are crusty on the outside. They are soft on the inside.

What is family life like in France?

When parents are not at work, families spend time together. Many parents and children in France come home for lunch. Families watch TV, read magazines and books, or visit museums. Relatives visit each other on Sundays and holidays.

What are the ethnic backgrounds of people in France?

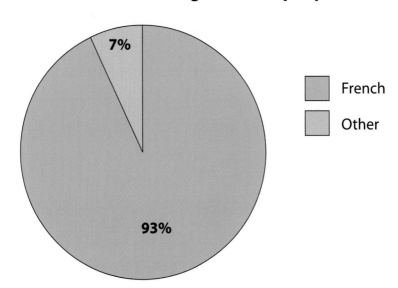

7%

93%

French

Other

Many families visit beaches during their summer vacations.

People in France have five weeks of vacation each year. Families take long trips. They visit beaches in summer and mountains in winter.

France Fast Facts

Official name:

French Republic

Land area:

210,668 square miles
(545,630 square kilometers)

Average annual precipitation:

26 inches (66 centimeters)

Average January temperature:

42 degrees Fahrenheit
(5.6 degrees Celsius)

Average July temperature:

76 degrees Fahrenheit
(24 degrees Celsius)

Population:

60,180,529 people

Capital city:

Paris

Language:

French

Natural resources:

bauxite, forests, uranium

Religions:

Roman Catholic	84%
Islamic	8%
Protestant	2%
Jewish	1%
Other	5%

Money and Flag

Money:

France's money is the euro. In 2004, 1 U.S. dollar equaled .8 euro. One Canadian dollar equaled .6 euro.

Flag:

The French flag is known as the French Tricolor. It has three vertical stripes of blue, white, and red. White is the color of the king. Blue and red are the colors of Paris.

Learn to Speak French

People in France speak French. It is France's official language. Learn to speak some French using the words below.

English	French	Pronunciation
good morning or good day	bonjour	(bohn-JOOR)
good-bye	au revoir	(OH ruh-VWAH)
good	bon	(BOHN)
great	grand	(GRAHN)
please	s'il vous plaît	(SEE VOO PLAY)
thank you	merci	(mare-SEE)
sorry	désolé	(day-zoh-LAY)
yes	oui	(WEE)
no	non	(NOH)

Glossary

economy (i-KON-uh-mee)—the way a country runs its industry, trade, and finance

parliament (PAR-luh-muhnt)—the group of people who have been elected to make laws in some countries

plateau (pla-TOH)—an area of high, flat land

prime minister (PRIME MIN-uh-stur)—the leader of a government

republic (ri-PUHB-lik)—a government led by a president with officials elected by voters

revolution (rev-uh-LOO-shun)—an uprising by the people of a country in an attempt to change the country's system of government

Internet Sites

FactHound offers a safe, fun way to find Internet sites related to this book. All of the sites on FactHound have been researched by our staff.

Here's how:
1. Visit *www.facthound.com*
2. Type in this special code **0736826890** for age-appropriate sites. Or enter a search word related to this book for a more general search.
3. Click on the **Fetch It** button.

FactHound will fetch the best sites for you!

Read More

Connolly, Sean. *The French Revolution.* Witness to History. Chicago: Heinemann Library, 2003.

Klingel, Cynthia Fitterer, and Robert B. Noyed. *France.* First Reports. Minneapolis: Compass Point Books, 2002.

Malone, Margaret Gay. *France.* Discovering Cultures. Tarrytown, N.Y. : Benchmark Books, 2003.

Mitten, Christopher. *France.* Steadwell Books World Tour. Austin, Texas: Raintree Steck-Vaughn, 2002.

Index